HOW TO MAKE
LIP BALM

A DIY Beginner's guide to creating and making your own lip balm

Legal & Disclaimer

The information contained in this book and its contents is not designed to replace or take the place of any form of medical or professional advice; and is not meant to replace the need for independent medical, financial, legal or other professional advice or services, as may be required. The content and information in this book has been provided for educational and entertainment purposes only.

The content and information contained in this book has been compiled from sources deemed reliable, and it is accurate to the best of the Author's knowledge, information, and belief. However, the Author cannot guarantee its accuracy and validity and cannot be held liable for any errors and/or omissions. Further, changes are periodically made to this book as and when needed. Where appropriate and/or necessary, you must consult a professional (including but not limited to your doctor, attorney, financial advisor or such other professional advisor) before using any of the suggested remedies, techniques, or information in this book.

Upon using the contents and information contained in this book, you agree to hold harmless the Author from and against any damages, costs, and expenses, including any legal fees potentially resulting from the application of any of the information provided by this book. This disclaimer applies to any loss, damages or injury caused by the use and application, whether directly or indirectly, of any advice or information presented, whether for breach of contract, tort, negligence, personal injury, criminal intent, or under any other cause of action.

You agree to accept all risks of using the information presented in this book.

You agree that by continuing to read this book, where appropriate and/or necessary, you shall consult a professional (including but not limited to your doctor, attorney, or financial advisor or such other advisor as needed) before using any of the suggested remedies, techniques, or information in this book.

Table of Contents

Introduction

Perhaps you are one of the many people who are vigilant about what you put in your body. You must have scoured grocery shelves for organic produce and products so that you don't dump harmful food additives, preservatives, and synthetic dyes into your body. But didn't you know that food isn't the only way to get toxins in your body? The thing is, your health does not only depend on your diet but also on what you apply on your skin.

But don't think that just because you are applying it onto your skin that it does not make its way into your bloodstream. Conventional beauty products contain a lot of substances that pose a lot of risks to human health. By virtue of osmosis, harmful chemicals applied to the skin gets absorbed and is directed to the tiny capillaries underneath the skin before they are circulated to the bloodstream. The side effects of include can range from minor to major complications such as allergic reactions, swelling, and redness to kidney damage, liver failure, and reproductive issues; respectively.

There has been countless news about commercial cosmetic brands containing harmful ingredients such as parabens, propylene glycol, butylated hydroxyanisole (BHA), sodium lauryl sulfate, phthalates, and butylated hydroxytoluene (BHT). Moreover, even synthetic mineral oil, fragrances, and flavors may also a cause side effect on the skin.

To make matters worse, FDA allows cosmetic manufacturers to lump together undisclosed ingredients as "fragrance" in order to protect trade secrets—and hide the dirty truth if you ask me.

Thus, this is the reason why it is crucial to learn how to make your own cosmetics. But, wait! Making your own cosmetics can be very ambitious especially if you don't even know anything about the art and science of cosmetic products. And so, I recommend that you start with a simple project–making your own lip balm.

When you make your own lip balm, you ensure that you are using natural and safe ingredients, so you don't put yourself at risk. Contrary to what most people think, making your own lip balm is very easy. It requires a few ingredients that you can easily find in stores and health shops. As a novice in making DIY cosmetics, starting with a lip balm is an easy project for you as it does not require complex ingredients and elaborate steps. As you get better, you can make different variations of lip balms. It may pique your interest even more to make other homemade cosmetics.

Lip balm first then your own line of homemade and organic cosmetics next.

Chapter 1
What You Need to Know About Lip Balms

The lips are the most vulnerable part of your face because the skin is so thin. This is the reason why it is the first to present signs of dryness and dehydration. This is the reason why lip balms are used. Also known as lip salve, lip balms are wax-like substances that are topically applied to the lips to moisturize dry or chapped lips. It is also used to treat other conditions such as cold sores, stomatitis, and angular cheilitis.

What It Does

The lips have a very unique nature. The skin on the lips is very thin and that the blood supply is close to the surface thus giving the lips its pink or reddish color. It also does not contain any oil glands unlike the rest of the skin thus it becomes easily dehydrated than the rest of your skin. Licking your lips to moisten it with saliva only provides temporary relief and it takes away the lips' natural moisture thus leaving it drier even more.

Once you apply salve on your lips, it provides an occlusive layer on the surface of the lip to seal moisture in and protect it from external exposure such as wind, dry air, and cold temperature. Since most lip balms are made from oil-based ingredients, the oil stays in place thus creating a protective layer. Lip balms can be applied directly to the lips using a finger, but you can also get them in a lipstick tube so that it can be applied directly to the lips.

The Humble Beginnings of Lip Balms

Lip balm is a ubiquitous product as you can easily find them in market shelves. But before the modern lip balm became popular, people have been using products to deal with chapped lips. Historical texts noted that people used animal fats, beeswax, nut butter, and natural butter to soften and moisturize their lips. Surprisingly, these are the same ingredients that we now use today to make lip balms.

The invention of lip balm was never possible if not for Robert Chesebrough–the inventor and patent owner for Vaseline. Later on, a physician, Charles Browne Fleet, from Lynchburg in Virginia invented the first lip balm which he then marketed the 1880s under his own company. The first lip balm was put in a small tin canister and it was only during 1936 when the tube-container was used to contain lip balms. The company Chapstick popularized this design that is still used until today.

But you will be interested–if not grossed out–to know that it used to contain traces of earwax. Before commercial lip bombs were made from beeswax, earwax was first used to treat cracked lips. In the book The American Frugal Housewife, earwax was used as the immediate home remedy to crack lips.

Issues on Conventional Lip Balms

Today, there are no longer lip balms that contain earwax – thank goodness! Many companies have created lip balms using ingredients you can find at home or in a DIY store. Popular brands of lip balms include Burt's Bees, Chapstick, Lypsyl, Blistex, Carmex, Labello, Tholene. And while most of these brands are deemed safe, some physicians have noted that some lip balms can cause more drying on the skin especially when it the use is discontinued. This is probably the reason why some people take note that lip balms can be addictive because they can't stop using them otherwise dryness on the lips becomes noticeable.

Commercial lip balms contain all sorts of ingredients from humectants (ingredients the help the skin hold on to moisture), emollients, and fragrances. But there are certain ingredients that can cause an allergic reaction to the skin. Many fragrances such as camphor and peppermint can cause drying and irritation of the skin. Moreover, emollients–particularly the oil-based ones–can cause irritation to people who have naturally oily skin.

The issues related to using commercial lip balms are the reasons why it might be more beneficial for you to make your own balm. By doing so, you will be able to add ingredients that you know will not cause adverse reactions to your skin.

Types of Lip Balms

There are different types of lip balms available in the market today. In fact, different lip balms are made for different purposes. This means that they are not only manufactured to moisturize the lips but also to address different medical concerns. Below are the types of lip balms that are available in the market. You can also use this list as a reference when making your own lip balms.

- **Lip balm with sunblock**: There are many lip balms that contain sunblock. This type of lip balm is great for people who spend long periods under the sun. Most lip balms with sunblock contain ingredients such as Vitamin E and Aloe Vera.

- **Flavored lip balm**: This type of lip balm is very popular especially among the younger users. They do not only moisturize the lips, but they also make wearing them fun. Popular flavors include strawberry, mint, cherry, and many others.

- **Medicinal lip balm**: This type of lip balm contains ingredients that can soothe pain on the lips especially those who suffered from intense damage. The ingredients of medicinal lip balm include camphor, menthol, phenol, and petrolatum to dull the pain and repair damaged lips.

Chapter 2
Lip Balm Basic Supplies

Lip balm is the easiest body care item that you can make as it requires only a few basic ingredients as well as supplies. Because the ingredients are simple, you can try adding more flavors as you become more confident with your lip balm-making skills. For this particular section, I will discuss the basic ingredients and supplies that you need when making lip balms.

The Core Ingredients

There are three core ingredients when making lip balms. The core ingredients refer to ingredients that are necessary when making lip balms. These ingredients are necessary for the integrity and quality of your lip balm. Without them, you won't be able to make lip balms at all. Below are the core ingredients that you need to stock up on if you want to make lip balms at home.

- **Body butter**: Body butter provides the moisturizing relief to dry lips. Select body butters that are hydrating and rich in Vitamin E as they provide not only protection but also anti-oxidants to make lips look younger. Examples of body butter that you can use in making lip balms include cocoa butter, shea butter, and mango butter. Cocoa butter is packed with Vitamin E. It is hydrating and smells chocolatey. Shea butter is also hydrating and is not only rich in Vitamin E but also in fatty acids for faster repair of the skin on your lips. Lastly, mango butter is rich in fatty acids and has ultra-moisturizing capabilities.

- **Emollient or nourishing oil**: Healthy oil is great for the skin as it provides additional moisture to the lips. There are different types of oils that you can use when making lip balms and these include almond oil, jojoba oil, avocado oil, apricot oil, and virgin coconut oil.

- **Beeswax**: Beeswax serves as the glue that that binds the body butter and oil together so that the resulting mixture is solid. But aside from binding the ingredients together, beeswax also comes with benefits to the skin. It provides a protective barrier to the skin and also helps soothe dry skin.

Other Ingredients

While the three ingredients are enough to make your very own lip balm, there are other value-adding ingredients that you can use so that you can make your lip balm more interesting. Below are the other ingredients that you can use when making lip balms.

- **Flavorings**: Make your lip balm more interesting by adding different types of flavor. Flavoring suggestions that you can use in making lip balms include peppermint, caramel, maple, coconut, Pina colada and many others. There are essential oils that you can use that will allow you to add flavor to your lip balm. Your imagination is your limit when it comes to adding flavor to lip balms. Some makers have made use of Kool-Aid juice mix to add color and flavor to your balms. Cocoa powder and cocoa powder can be used for a chocolate-flavored balm. Rose petals can be crushed as another flavoring option. The key is to make sure that whatever flavoring you add can last long and will not be a source of mold or bacteria.

- **Coloring**: While natural and colorless lip balm is great, adding color to your lip balm can add more color to your lips. Aside from using artificial color, you can use mica powder to add shimmer to your lip balm. Mica powder can be used on tinted and non-tinted lip balm to add shine to your gloss.

Beeswax Alternatives

While beeswax is considered as a core ingredient in making lip balm, what if you are a vegan or have allergic reactions to it? This does not mean that you should forgo using lip balms altogether because you cannot use beeswax. There are different alternatives that you can use if you don't like using beeswax.

- **Candelilla wax**: This type of wax is obtained from the leaves of the candelilla plant that is native to Mexico. It is used as a substitute for beeswax in making lip balms, lipsticks, lotions, creams, and soaps. This type of wax has lubricating properties but is less pliable and harder than beeswax. It also hardens faster than beeswax. If you are going to use this wax, use half of it as you would with beeswax so that you can work with it easily.

- **Carnauba wax**: Also called palm wax or Brazil wax, this type of wax is extracted by the Copernicia prunifera palm. It is used in combination with either candelilla wax or beeswax. If you use it by itself, make sure that you use less of it as you would with a beeswax because it hardens and solidifies fast.

- **Soy Wax**: Soy wax is a popular alternative to beeswax and is often preferred by vegan consumers. Unlike candelilla and carnauba wax, it is no harder than beeswax thus it can be used in equal amounts if you use it as a substitute for beeswax.

Basic Lip Balm Tools and Equipment

When making lip balms, it is important that you have dedicated tools that you should never use for other purposes. You can improvise and use ordinary kitchen tools and equipment especially if it is your first time to make lip balm. But as you develop skills, it is more beneficial if you invest in tools and equipment. Below are the basic tools that you will need when making lip balms.

- **Funnel pitcher**: A funnel pitcher makes it easy for you to mix and pour the mixture into lip tubes and tins. They often come with graduations, so it is easy to achieve precise measuring of ingredients into containers.

- **Measuring cups**: Measuring cups allow you to measure ingredients precisely. Make sure that you opt for those made from natural HDPE plastic as they can withstand essential and fragrance oils.

- **Melting pot**: Use this equipment to melt small batches of lip balms base. While there are melting pots that are made for such purpose, you don't have to buy one especially if you are still starting out. What you can do is to get two pots of different sizes. Put water in the bigger pot and place the smaller one on top of the water to create a double boiler.

- **Whisk**: A whisk will help you mix all ingredients thoroughly. You can use other tools to mix your ingredients such as a stirring rod or an ordinary wooden stick, but the whisk is able to mix everything together more efficiently.

- **Safety gears**: Since you will be working with hot wax constantly when making lip balms, you need to wear safety gears at all times. These include goggles, gloves, and an apron.

- **Digital scale**: A scale is necessary for you to accurately measure the ingredients. Choose scales that can read at least two decimal places.

- **Silicone spatula**: Silicone spatula is perfect for mixing lip balm bases because it is easy to clean. Moreover, it can also withstand high heat from the melted body butter. If you don't have a spatula, you can also use a silicone scraper for scraping bowls and jars.

- **Pipette**: This tool allows you to transfer the hot lip balm mixture into lip balm tubes or tins.

- **Lip balm tubes or tins**: Lip balm tubes or tins are used to store the finished product. Choose one that fits your style and preferences.

Chapter 3
Basic Steps to Make Lip Balm

As I have mentioned earlier, there are so many recipes of lip balms that you can try but before you get your hands on the more complicated stuff, make sure that you get yourself familiar with the steps on making a simple lip balm recipe. This chapter will teach you just that.

Preparation

The first that you need to do is to prepare the ingredients and the equipment. The focus of this chapter is to teach you how to make a simple 5-ingredient peppermint lip balm. As you get the gist of it, you can add more ingredients and improvise to make a lip balm with your own personal touch.

1. Prepare the equipment

For this project, I used a small Corelle bowl, muffin tins, spatula, 1 tablespoon measuring spoon, empty lip-gloss tubes, and a glass pipette with rubber ball.

2. Prepare the Ingredients

For this recipe, you will need the following:

- 2 tablespoons beeswax chopped or grated

- 2 tablespoons avocado oil

- 2 tablespoons almond oil

- 1 tablespoon shea butter

- 8 drops peppermint pure essential oil

Mixing the Wax and Oils

1. Measure and melt the beeswax

I used both a muffin tin on low fire to melt the beeswax. This only takes no more than two minutes to melt. Please, it is important to only use the lowest fire setting.

If using a double boiler, this is how it should look. Place a large pan with an inch of water on medium fire. And then in the middle of the pan, place a small pot where you will melt your wax.

2. Measure and add the shea butter into the melted beeswax

Still using the same muffin tin, add the one tablespoon of shea butter into the melted beeswax and melt on low fire. This will take around two minutes. Stirring with your rubber spatula to ensure that nothing gets burned and all the shea butter melts and mixes well with the beeswax.

3. Stir in the other oils, avocado and almond.

At this point, I have turned off the fire. Poured in two tablespoons each of avocado oil and almond oil. Stirred with my spatula to mix well. If you are using coloring, this is the point where you add it.

4. Transferred mixture into a heatproof bowl

This step can be skipped if your muffin tin is quite big. Unfortunately for me, after adding the oils it was near to overflowing that I can't stir the mixture properly.

Heatproof bowl is important because at some point you need to turn on the fire to stop the mixture from solidifying.

5. Add the essential oil

I usually add the fragrance and essential oils last. Mix well.

Transfer to A Container

1. Ready the lip balm tubes

This is an important step because the tubes need to be in an upright position. What I did was place them in muffin tins to ensure that when one falls, they don't fall on the other tubes and cause a domino effect. And the messiness is contained within the tins. If you have a lip balm tube holder or lipstick holder that would also work here.

2. Use a Pipette to transfer mixture into tubes

I cannot emphasize the importance of a pipette. You have to buy one or need to have one with a rubber bulb. Without a pipette, the lip balm making process is going to drive you nuts. This is especially because one tube can contain as much as 5-mL of lip balm mixture and a medicine dropper can just hold at the most 1-mL.

Further, the lip balm mixture can solidify quite fast. With a pipette, if it solidifies, then it doesn't come out. This is easily remedied by running the glass pipette on fire. You can see the mixture going from opaque to translucent and this will make it easier to pour it into tubes.

You also have to consider that with this recipe alone, I was able to fill 15 tubes of lip balm. If you're going to use a medicine dropper, it's not convenient. And if the mixture solidifies inside, you're lucky if it is a glass dropper and you can run it over a fire. But, if it's a plastic medicine dropper, you can't.

3. Allow to solidify

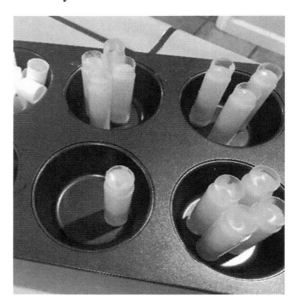

Just leave the filled tubes uncovered for at least 5 minutes to solidify. Try not to move them to keep the top of the balm leveled.

4. Cover and label

This is the last step of the process. Before you put a cap on the tubes, make sure to wipe it carefully of any drippings with a paper towel.

Chapter 4
More Advanced Lip Balm Recipes

Making your own lip balm is a fun activity. Now that you have learned about how to make basic lip balms, it is time to try your hands on making advanced lip balm recipes. Thus, this chapter will teach you how to make all sorts of lip balm to fit your needs.

Tinted Lip Balm

Make tinted lip balms using simple ingredients so that you do not only moisturize your lips, but you also add color to them.

Yields approximately: 27 tubes

Ingredients:

- 4 tablespoons beeswax
- 4 tablespoons cocoa butter
- 4 tablespoons coconut oil
- 1 ½ teaspoons iron oxide

Instructions:

1. In a double boiler or melt pot, mix together beeswax, cocoa butter, and coconut oil.

2. Melt over medium heat while stirring constantly to combine all ingredients.

3. Stir in the iron oxide once the oil and beeswax have melted. Mix until well-combined.

4. Test the lip balm if you have achieved the desired tint. Add more iron oxide for a redder tint.

5. Use a pipette to place in lip balm tins or tubes.

6. Allow to cool before using.

Lip Balm W/ SPF

Wear this lip balm on a hot and sunny day. Raspberry seed oil has a natural sun protection factor of 28-50.

Yields approximately: 13 tubes

Ingredients:

- 2 tablespoons coconut oil

- 1 tablespoon olive oil

- 5 wafers of cocoa butter shredded

- 1 ½ tablespoons beeswax, chopped

- 1 teaspoon raspberry seed oil

- 15 drops of your favorite essential oil

Instructions:

1. Melt coconut oil, olive oil, cocoa butter, and beeswax in a double boiler until melted.

2. Remove from the heat and add the red raspberry seed oil and essential oils.

3. While still warm, use a pipette to fill lip balm tubes with the mixture.

4. Allow to cool before using.

Coconut Oil Lip Balm

Coconut oil is not only touted for its moisturizing quality, but it also has anti-inflammatory effects thus this DIY lip balm is great for people who suffer from severe chapped lips.

Yields approximately: 15 tubes

Ingredients:

- 2 tablespoons coconut oil, organic

- 2 tablespoons jojoba oil

- 2 tablespoons beeswax

- 1 tablespoon Shea butter

Instructions:

1. In a double boiler, melt all ingredients over medium heat.

2. Once melted, turn off the heat.

3. Use a pipette to transfer the mixture into lip tint tubes.

4. Allow to set in the fridge before using.

Cocoa Butter Lip Balm

This simple cocoa butter lip balm is made more interesting with its chocolatey flavor. It is an addictive lip balm that you will want to put on your lips again and again.

Yields approximately: 14 tubes

Ingredients:

- 1 ½ tablespoons beeswax

- 2 tablespoons cocoa butter

- 3 tablespoons sweet almond oil

- 10 drops vanilla oil

- 8 drops vitamin E oil

Instructions:

1. Place the beeswax, cocoa butter, and sweet almond oil in a double boiler.

2. Heat under medium flame until the mixture has melted completely.

3. Turn the heat to low and add vanilla and Vitamin E oil.

4. Mix until well-combined.

5. Use a pipette to transfer the contents into lip balm tins or tubes.

Rose Lip Balm

This calming lip balm has rose essences to it that will not only moisturize your lips but will also give you a feel of elegance and sophistication.

Yields approximately: 24 tubes

Ingredients:

- 4 tablespoons beeswax grated

- 4 tablespoons coconut oil

- 2 tablespoons almond oil

- 14 drops of rose essential oil

- 1 tablespoon rose water

Instructions:

1. In a double boiler, add the beeswax, coconut oil, and almond oil.

2. Heat over medium and allow to melt.

3. Once melted, reduce the heat to low and add rose essential oil and rose water.

4. Whisk until well combined.

5. Use a pipette or a medicine dropper and transfer the mixture into lip balm tubes.

6. Allow to harden before using.

Shea Butter Lip Balm

This Shea butter lip balm recipe will moisturize your lips for a longer time. It Is easy to make and does not require a lot of ingredients.

Yields approximately: 27 tubes

Ingredients:

- 4 tablespoons Shea butter
- 4 tablespoons beeswax
- 4 tablespoons coconut oil
- 1 teaspoon honey
- 20 drops lemon balm essential oil
- 5 drops chamomile essential oil
- 4 drops orange essential oil

Instructions:

1. In a double boiler over medium flame, heat the Shea butter, beeswax, and coconut oil until melted.

2. Reduce the heat to low and add honey and the essential oils

3. Mix to combine.

4. Turn off the heat and Use a pipette to transfer into lip balm tubes.

5. Allow to harden and set in the fridge for a few minutes before using.

Colored Lip Balm

Use this recipe to make endless variations of colored lip balms. Just substitute to the color that you want, and you are good to go.

Yields approximately: 10 tubes

Ingredients:

- 2 tablespoons coconut oil

- 1 tablespoon beeswax

- 1 tablespoon Shea butter

- ½ teaspoon white mica powder

- 1 teaspoon lip-safe iron oxide powder (any color that you want)

Ingredients:

1. In a double boiler over medium heat, melt the coconut, beeswax, and Shea butter.

2. Once melted, reduce the heat to low and whisk in the mica powder and iron oxide.

3. Mix until well combined.

4. Use a pipette to transfer into individual containers.

Flavored Lip Balm

Flavored lip balms are fun to wear. This flavored lip balm recipe will definitely make you want to regularly use it.

Yields approximately: 13 tubes

Ingredients:

- ¼ cup freeze-dried fruits of your choice
- 1 tablespoon beeswax grated
- ½ tablespoon coconut oil
- ½ tablespoon sweet almond oil
- ⁺ teaspoon Vitamin E oil

Instructions:

1. Put the freeze-dried fruits in a blender and pulse until it becomes a fine powder. Set aside.

2. Place all the ingredients including the powdered strawberries in a heat-safe glass container.

3. Put the container of ingredients inside a pan with boiling water. Make sure that the water comes halfway up the side of the container. Be careful not to get any water into the mixture.

4. Allow the water to simmer and stir the mixture occasionally with a stirring rod or spatula.

5. Remove the jar from the water and pass the mixture through a strainer. Discard the solids.

6. Transfer into lip balm tubes and allow to set for a few minutes.

Vitamin E Lip Balm

Nourish your skin with this Vitamin E lip balm recipe so that you will look youthful and glowing at all times.

Yields approximately: 28 tubes

Ingredients:

- 4 tablespoons beeswax

- 4 tablespoons Shea butter

- 4 tablespoons avocado oil

- 1 tablespoon vitamin E oil

- 4 drops rose geranium essential oil

Instructions:

1. In a double boiler over medium heat, melt the beeswax, Shea butter, and avocado oil until melted.

2. Once melted, turn off the heat and stir in Vitamin E oil and essential oil. Whisk to combine.

3. Pour into lip balm tins or pipette into lip balm tubes.

Honey Lip Balm

This sweet and moisturizing honey lip balm is just what you need on a hot summer day. It is easy to make yet provides extra moisture on your skin all throughout the day.

Yields approximately: 8 tubes

Ingredients:

- 4 teaspoons beeswax pellets

- 3 teaspoons organic coconut oil

- 3 teaspoons sunflower seed oil

- 1 teaspoon liquid honey

- 5 drops peppermint essential oil

Instructions:

1. In a double boiler over medium heat, melt the beeswax, coconut oil, sunflower seed oil, and honey.

2. Stir to combine everything.

3. Once melted, reduce the heat to low and whisk in essential oil. Stir to combine.

4. Use a pipette to transfer into individual containers.

Aloe Vera Lip Balm

This refreshing aloe Vera lip balm will not only moisturize your lips, but it will also address other issues on your lips such as reducing inflammation and itchiness.

Yields approximately: 8 tubes

Ingredients:

- ½ tablespoon beeswax

- 1 ½ tablespoons coconut oil

- 1 teaspoon cocoa butter

- 1 teaspoon aloe Vera gel

- 10 drops of vitamin E oil

- 8 drops of essential oil of your choice

Instructions:

1. In a double boiler, melt the beeswax, coconut oil, and cocoa butter. Heat over medium flame.

2. Once melted, turn the heat to low and add in the aloe Vera gel, vitamin E oil, and essential oil. Stir to combine all ingredients then turn off the heat.

3. Use medicine dropper and transfer into lip balm tubes or tins.

Peppermint Lip Balm

Peppermint lip balm does not only moisturize your lips, but it also has cooling effect that will last for a long time. It is a refreshing lip balm recipe that you need to give a try.

Yields approximately: 30 tubes

Ingredients:

- 4 tablespoons beeswax pellets

- 4 tablespoons coconut oil

- 6 tablespoons sweet almond oil

- 10 drops peppermint oil

Instructions:

1. In a double boiler, heat the beeswax, coconut oil, and almond oil until melted.

2. Turn off the heat and add peppermint oil.

3. Transfer to lip balm tubes using a pipette or medicine dropper.

4. Allow to set and harden in the fridge before using.

Strawberry Lip Balm

This delicious strawberry-flavored lip balm will definitely make your day. Make several tubes of this lip balm and give them away to friends and family to brighten their day.

Yields approximately: 22 tubes

Ingredients:

- 4 tablespoons Shea butter

- 2 tablespoons beeswax

- 4 tablespoons rosehip seed oil

- 4 drops pure strawberry extract

- 1 teaspoon mica powder

Instructions:

1. In a double boiler over medium heat, melt the Shea butter, beeswax, and rosehip seed oil.

2. Once melted, reduce the heat to low and add in the strawberry extract and mica powder.

3. Whisk until well-combined.

4. Use a pipette and transfer into lip balm tubes or tins.

5. Allow to harden in the fridge for 2 hours before using.

Mint Lip Balm

This minty lip balm adds refreshing feeling to your lips. It is a perfect lip balm to wear on a warm day as it provides extra moisture and coolness to your lips.

Yields approximately: 5 tubes

Ingredients:

- 2 teaspoons white beeswax pellets
- 2 teaspoons coconut oil
- 2 teaspoons sweet almond oil
- 2 drops peppermint oil

Instructions:

1. Melt the beeswax in a double boiler over medium flame.
2. Stir in the coconut oil and sweet almond oil.
3. Turn off the heat and add the peppermint oil last.
4. Pour into small containers.
5. Allow to set for a few hours before using.

Olive Oil Lip Balm

Olive oil has great moisturizing abilities. Moreover, it also helps improve the quality of the skin. This recipe is great for extremely damaged lips.

Yields approximately: 17 tubes

Ingredients:

- 3 tablespoons extra virgin olive oil
- 3 tablespoons beeswax
- 1 tablespoon Shea butter
- ½ teaspoon Vitamin E oil
- 1 teaspoon honey
- 15 drops peppermint essential oil

Instructions:

1. In a double boiler over medium heat, melt the olive oil, beeswax, and Shea butter. Use a spatula and stir.

2. Once melted, reduce the heat to low and add the Vitamin E oil, honey, and peppermint essential oil. Stir to combine everything.

3. Pour into lip balm tubes or tins.

4. Allow to set in the fridge before using.

Vanilla Lip Balm

Anything vanilla flavored is exciting including this lip balm recipe. This recipe does not only help soothe chapped lips but also refreshes your feeling because of its delicious aroma.

Yields approximately: 32 tubes

Ingredients:

- 4 ½ tablespoons avocado oil

- 4 tablespoons Shea butter

- 4 tablespoons beeswax grated

- 2 tablespoons coconut oil

- 1 teaspoon Vitamin E oil

- 2 drops vanilla extract

Instructions:

1. In a double boiler, melt the avocado oil, Shea butter, beeswax, and coconut oil.

2. Blend until well combined.

3. Once melted, reduce the heat to low and add Vitamin E oil and vanilla extract.

4. Pour into lip balm tins or pipette into tubes.

5. Allow to set and harden before using.

Lavender Lip Balm

This lavender lip balm recipe gives you a relaxing feeling. This recipe is easy to make as long as you have the main ingredient – lavender oil!

Yields approximately: 9 tubes

Ingredients:

- 1 tablespoon coconut oil

- 1 tablespoon beeswax

- 2 tablespoons Shea butter

- 7 drops lavender essential oil

Instructions:

1. In a double boiler, heat the oil, beeswax, and Shea butter until melted.

2. Once melted, turn off the heat and add in the lavender essential oil.

3. Use a pipette to transfer the mixture into lip balm tubes or tins.

4. Allow to harden before using.

Banana Lip Balm

This fruity lip balm recipe will surely invigorate your day. Made from the basic lip balm ingredients and banana extract, everyone in your family will definitely like this lip balm.

Yields approximately: 23 tubes

Ingredients:

- 4 tablespoons beeswax grated
- 2 tablespoons almond oil
- 2 tablespoons coconut oil
- 2 tablespoons Shea butter
- 1 teaspoon banana essential oil
- 1 teaspoon Vitamin E oil

Instructions:

1. In a double boiler, heat the beeswax, almond oil, coconut oil, and Shea butter until melted.

2. Reduce the heat once melted and add in the banana essential oil and Vitamin E oil.

3. Whisk to combine everything.

4. Transfer into lip balm tubes.

5. Allow to set and harden before using.

Watermelon Lip Balm

This refreshing watermelon lip balm recipe is perfect for the summer months. And just like other DIY lip balm recipes, this one is easy to do as well.

Yields approximately: 23 tubes

Ingredients:

- 4 tablespoons beeswax grated
- 2 tablespoons grapeseed oil
- 2 tablespoons coconut oil
- 2 tablespoons cocoa butter
- 1 teaspoon watermelon essential oil
- 1 teaspoon Vitamin E oil

Instructions:

1. In a double boiler, heat the beeswax, grapeseed oil, coconut oil, and cocoa butter until melted.

2. Reduce the heat once melted and add in the watermelon essential oil and Vitamin E oil.

3. Whisk to combine everything then transfer into lip balm tubes.

4. Allow to set and harden before using.

Chocolate Lip Balm

This chocolate lip balm recipe is delicious enough to eat. You will be addicted to put it on your lips all the time.

Yields approximately: 13 tubes

Ingredients:

- 3 tablespoons beeswax chopped
- 1 ½ tablespoons coconut oil
- 1 tablespoon cocoa butter
- 1 teaspoon cocoa powder

Instructions:

1. Heat a double boiler over medium flame.
2. Melt the beeswax, coconut oil and cocoa butter.
3. Reduce the heat once melted and stir in the cocoa powder until well-combined.
4. Use a pipette and transfer into lip balm tubes.
5. Allow to harden and set inside the fridge for a few minutes before using.

Shimmer Lip Balm

Add a glamorous appeal to your lips with this shimmer lip balm recipe. You will definitely attract the right attention with this simple recipe.

Yields approximately: 7 tubes

Ingredients:

- 1 tablespoon Shea butter
- 1 tablespoon coconut oil
- 1 tablespoon beeswax pastilles
- ½ teaspoons mica powder
- 15 drops of peppermint essential oil

Instructions:

1. In a double boiler over medium flame, heat the Shea butter, coconut oil, ad beeswax.

2. Once melted, lower the heat to low and stir in the mica powder and peppermint essential oil.

3. Transfer to lip balm tubes or tins and allow to set or harden before using.

Glossy Lip Balm

This glossy lip balm recipe will not only moisturize your lips, but it will also make it look luscious and healthy.

Yields approximately: 20 tubes

Ingredients:

- 5 tablespoons extra virgin coconut oil

- 4 tablespoons beeswax

- 1 ½ teaspoons Vitamin E oil

- 25 drops peppermint essential oil

Instructions:

1. Heat a double boiler over medium flame.

2. Melt the coconut oil and beeswax.

3. Reduce the heat once melted and stir in vitamin E oil and peppermint essential oil.

4. Use a pipette and transfer into lip balm tubes.

5. Allow to harden and set inside the fridge for a few minutes before using.

Orange Lip Balm

This citrusy and refreshing lip balm is what you need on a warm sunny day. It has a very nice aroma thus it does not only make your lips look moisturized, but you can also use it as part of your aromatherapy routine.

Yields approximately: 38 tubes

Ingredients:

- 8 tablespoons beeswax

- 8 tablespoons coconut oil

- 1 ½ tablespoons honey

- 30 drops sweet orange essential oil

Instructions:

1. Heat a double boiler over medium flame.

2. Melt the beeswax, coconut oil, and honey.

3. Once melted, reduce the heat to low and add the orange essential oil.

4. Mix to combine.

5. Transfer to lip balm tubes or tins.

Mango Lip Balm

This tropical-flavored lip balm will give your lips an exotic feel. And since it contains castor oil, you also get the anti-inflammatory benefits especially if you suffer from extremely dry lips. This is a great gift idea to those who collect interesting flavors of lip balms.

Yields approximately: 4 tubes

Ingredients:

- ½ teaspoon Shea butter

- ½ teaspoon mango butter

- 2 teaspoon sweet almond oil

- 1 teaspoon castor oil

- 1 teaspoon beeswax

- 4 drops lavender essential oil

- ¼ teaspoon Vitamin E oil

- 1 drop tea tree oil

Instructions:

1. In a double boiler, place the Shea butter, mango butter, sweet almond oil, castor oil, and beeswax.

2. Allow to melt while stirring constantly.

3. Once melted, reduce the heat to low and add in the essential oil, vitamin E oil, and tea tree oil.

4. Whisk to combine.

5. Turn off the heat and transfer to lip balm tins or tubes while still warm.

Almond Oil Lip Balm

This recipe is simple and very basic. Nevertheless, this is a perfect lip balm recipe for those who want a no-fuss recipe that is effective in resolving dry and chapped lips.

Yields approximately: 9 tubes

Ingredients:

- 1 tablespoon almond oil

- 2 tablespoons beeswax

- 1 tablespoon honey

Instructions:

1. In a double boiler, heat the almond oil and beeswax until melted. Stir constantly.

2. Once melted, reduce the heat to low and add honey. Whisk to combine.

3. Turn off the heat and transfer to lip balm tins or tubes while still warm.

Dr. Pepper Lip Balm

This whimsical lip balm has the flavor of your favorite Dr. Pepper's soda. It will surely be a hit among the younger users but will definitely have fans across generations.

Yields approximately: 26 tubes

Ingredients:

- 8 tablespoons almond oil

- 2 tablespoons beeswax

- 4 teaspoons honey

- 1 pack black cherry Kool-Aid

- ½ teaspoon pure vanilla extract

- 5 drops orange essential oil

- 5 drops clove essential oil

- 10 drops cinnamon essential oil

Instructions:

1. In a double boiler, combine the almond oil, beeswax, and honey. Set over medium heat.

2. Add in the cherry Kool-Aid and mix until incorporated and everything has blended well.

3. Turn off the heat and add the rest of the ingredients.

4. Use a pipette to transfer to lip balm tubes.

Organic Lip Balm

Lip balms made from organic ingredients are good for the health. This recipe is for the health conscious.

Yields approximately: 45 tubes

Ingredients:

- ¼ cup sweet almond oil, organic

- ¼ cup Shea butter, organic

- ¾ cup beeswax

- 5 drops of essential oil

- 1 teaspoon powdered beet root

Instructions:

1. In a double boiler, combine the almond oil, Shea butter, and beeswax. Set over medium heat.

2. Turn off the heat and add the rest of the ingredients.

3. Use a pipette to transfer to lip balm tubes.

4. Allow to set or harden before using.

Lime Lip Balm

This refreshing lip balm recipe has a citrus flavor and is jam-packed with antioxidants to protect your lips from chapping and drying.

Yields approximately: 9 tubes

Ingredients:

- 2 tablespoons coconut oil

- 2 teaspoons cocoa butter

- 2 teaspoons beeswax

- 2 teaspoons almond oil

- 1-5 drops of lime essential oil

Instructions:

1. In a double boiler over medium heat, combine the coconut oil, cocoa butter, beeswax, and almond oil until melted.

2. Turn off the heat and add the lime essential oil.

3. Whisk until combined.

4. Transfer to lip balm tubes or tins and allow to harden for a few hours before using.

Coconut Rose Lip Balm

A perfect combination of coconut and rose petals, this refreshing lip balm is very easy to make. Make sure that you have both ingredients – coconut oil and rose petals–to make this whimsical recipe.

Yields approximately: 27 tubes

Ingredients:

- $^{1}/_{8}$ cup coconut oil

- ¼ cup beeswax, grated or chopped

- $^{1}/_{8}$ cup Shea butter

- 1 teaspoon coconut or vanilla extract

- ¼ cup rose petals

- 1 teaspoon sweet almond oil

Instructions:

1. Place all ingredients in a heat-proof glass and put in a microwave oven for 30 seconds.

2. If the mixture has not melted yet, place in a microwave oven for another 30 seconds.

3. Mix until well combined.

4. Pour through a sieve to strain the rose petals.

5. Pour into lip balm tubes or tins and allow to harden for a few minutes.

Honey Orange Vanilla Lip Balm

A tasty and aromatic lip balm that is great for summer, this honey, orange, and vanilla lip balm will definitely excite you to use it every day.

Yields approximately: 11 tubes

Ingredients:

- 2 tablespoons beeswax
- ½ teaspoon raw honey
- 3 tablespoons coconut oil
- 15 drops each of orange and vanilla essential oils

Instructions:

1. In a double boiler, place the beeswax, honey, and coconut oil.
2. Whisk until well combined.
3. Once melted, turn off the heat and stir in the orange and vanilla essential oils.
4. Pour immediately into lip balm tubes and tins.
5. Allow to harden inside the fridge before using.

Raspberry Lip Balm

This luscious and delicious lip balm recipe is made more interesting with raspberry extract. You can also substitute raspberry to other berries such as blueberries and blackberry.

Yields approximately: 6 tubes

Ingredients:

- 2 tablespoons coconut oil

- ½ tablespoon ground and freeze-dried raspberries

- 1 teaspoon beeswax

Instructions:

1. In a double boiler, place coconut oil, raspberries, and beeswax.

2. Whisk until well combined.

3. Once melted, turn off the heat and pour immediately into lip balm tubes and tins.

4. Allow to harden inside the fridge before using.

Lip Balm with Castor Oil

This lip balm ingredient contains castor oil that has anti-inflammatory properties thus making this recipe perfect for people who suffer from extremely dry lips.

Yields approximately: 14 tubes

Ingredients:

- 2 tablespoons coconut oil
- 2 tablespoons beeswax
- 1 tablespoon Shea butter
- 1 tablespoon castor oil
- 1 teaspoon zinc oxide
- 7 drops peppermint essential oil
- 7 drops lavender essential oil

Instructions:

1. In a double boiler, melt the coconut oil, beeswax, Shea butter, and castor oil.
2. Use a whisk or stirring rod to combine everything.
3. Once melted, reduce the heat to low and add in the zinc oxide and essential oils.
4. Stir to combine everything.
5. Use a medicinal dropper to transfer to lip balm tubes and tins.
6. Allow to harden and set inside the fridge before using them.

Pink Grapefruit Lip Balm

Grapefruit contains potent amounts of Vitamin C. Its citrusy smell makes it perfect for the hot summer months.

Yields approximately: 15 tubes

Ingredients:

- 2 tablespoons beeswax grated or chopped
- 1 tablespoons Shea butter
- 2 tablespoons coconut oil
- 1 tablespoon castor oil
- ½ teaspoon grapefruit essential oil
- ½ teaspoon powdered beet root, fine
- 1 teaspoon grape juice

Instructions:

1. In a small saucepan over low flame, place the beeswax, Shea butter, coconut oil, and castor oil.
2. Stir using a stirring rod.
3. Once melted, remove the pan from the heat and ass the rest of the ingredients.
4. Use a whisk to combine everything.
5. Use a medicinal dropper or pipette to transfer into lip balm tubes or tins.

Chapter 5
Resources and Supplies

The ingredients to make lip balms are ubiquitous and they are found in many health stores. But how do you know that you bought quality grade ingredients? Buying the ingredients to make lip balms may sound easy but if you want the best results for your DIY creations, it is vital that you know how and where to buy the right ingredients. Below is a guide on where to get high-grade ingredients to make different recipes for lip balms.

Beeswax

Beeswax is the most important ingredient when making lip balms. It is important to take note that there are different variations or preparations of beeswax. In most cases, you get a beeswax block, which comes in chunks instead of a single block. The challenge with working with large chunks of beeswax is that you need to grate or chop it yourself when making lip balms. Thus, another solution is to get the beeswax pellets. Each pellet has the precise size so there is no need for you to shave from a single block. Moreover, it also melts faster and easier than block or chunks of beeswax. Aside from beeswax pellets, you can also get beeswax sheets as it melts faster like the pellets.

When buying beeswax to make lip balms, it is crucial that you ask about the presence of impurities. Most lip balms sold in the market are tainted with pesticide residues that the bees encountered while they are foraging for food. In most cases, pesticides are intentionally introduced into the hive to destroy pests like the Varroa mites. The thing is that you don't want your lips to come into contact with something that is dangerous to the health. As such, it is crucial to get beeswax that is either organic or pharmaceutical grade.

There are many places where you can buy beeswax. If there are no health stores around you, your best option is to get them online. There are many places online where you can buy beeswax but what matters is that you check the reputation of the online retailer to ensure that your beeswax is organic. Another option – but nevertheless better – is to get your beeswax from a local beekeeper. Not only does it help the local beekeeping industry in your area, but you can also be assured of the source of your beeswax. So, if you have a neighborhood beekeeper, be friends with them.

Body Butter

Body buttes can help nourish your skin from the inside out. There are different types of body butter that you can use but it is important to take note that each has different benefits for different skin types. For instance, cocoa butter that is obtained from the cacao bean pod can help in scar relief thus making it great for extremely chapped lips while shea butter contains high amounts of Vitamins A and E as well as collagen to make the lips look suppler. It also has natural SPF thus making it a perfect ingredient for making lip balms with UV protection. Mango butter, on the other hand, has high moisturizing qualities.

When buying body butters, make sure that you choose those that are pure and organic. There are many places where you can buy body butters. You can try your local health stores as they usually stock up on body butters. You can also get them online as there are many online retail stores that carry different brands of body butters.

Emollient Oils

Emollient oils refer to natural vegetable oils that are necessary for providing moisture on the skin. These include coconut oil, olive oil, sweet almond oil, jojoba oil, and other carrier oils. Among the other ingredients in making lip balms, emollient oils are the easiest to find. For instance, you can buy olive oil and coconut oil in grocery stores while sweet almond oil, jojoba, and other carrier oils are usually sold in health stores. You can also buy them from online retail stores but make sure that the seller has a good reputation. When buying emollient oils, it is important to choose those that are food grade because they are safe to use in making cosmetics particularly lip balms.

Essential Oils

Essential oils give lip balms aroma and additional therapeutic benefits. When buying essential oils, make sure that you test the oils first to ensure that they are real essential oils. It is important to get high-quality essential oils. Avoid the cheap imitation oils because they might contain synthetic ingredients and chemicals that can pose negative effects to the body. When you buy essential oils, get them from local natural food stores that sell real essential oils such as brands like Doterra and Young Living as they are certified essential oils.

Since essential oils are expensive, make sure that you buy certified essential oils that you will likely use all the time. Essential oils that are commonly used in making lip balms include lavender, peppermint, vanilla, and orange.

Color

The coloring is an important ingredient in making lip balms. They do not only make the finished products look attractive, but they also add extra color to your lips so that you stand out while having your lips moisturized. The most common way to color lip balms is by using powdered micas. Micas are naturally-occurring minerals that can range from opalescent to matte. They are often sold by weight and not in volume thus it is crucial to determine how much you need to make your lip balm.

Other types of colorants that you can use when making lip balms include oxides and pigments. While mica powders only produce warm colors on the lip balm, oxides and other natural pigments can produce a wide variety of colors. Finding these colorants can be difficult as you cannot buy them from ordinary grocery stores. However, there are many online stores that sell good quality powdered mica that you can use when making lip balms.

Conclusion

Everyone should have their own tube of lip balm stashed in their vanity kit. The thing is that you don't need to buy your own lip balm after reading this eBook. You can make your own lip balm that can benefit the specific condition of your lips. The best thing about making your own lip balm is that you know what goes in it thus you know that it is safe and effective in treating chapped lips. Moreover, you don't need to obtain any special skills so that you can make them. You can also rely on your creativity so that you can make a batch of lip balms that you can give to your friends and family. They will definitely love the idea of receiving a tube of lip balm from you. After following the recipes in this book, your skills will greatly improve so you can make your very own creation of lip balms. Have fun in making lip balms and good luck!

If you've enjoyed reading this book, subscribe* to my mailing list for exclusive content and sneak peaks of my future books.

Click the link below:
http://eepurl.com/dCTyG1

OR

Use the QR Code:

(*Must be 13 years or older to subscribe)

Printed in Great Britain
by Amazon